"MY PARENT HAS A BRAIN INJURY..."

...a Guide for Young People

by Jo Johnson
Consultant Neuropsychologist

Illustrated by Lauren Densham

First published in Great Britain November 2011

ISBN 978-0-9557588-3-6

Item: MPBI

Published by Lash & Associates Publishing/Training Inc.
100 Boardwalk Drive, Suite 150, Youngsville, NC 27596
Tel: (919) 556-0300

This book is part of a series on brain injury among children, adolescents, adults and veterans. For a free catalog, contact Lash & Associates
Tel: (919) 556-0300 or visit our web site www.lapublishing.com

A big *thank you* to all the young
people who have contributed to this
book and to the professionals, who
read several drafts and provided
constructive feedback.

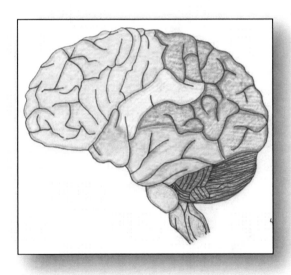

About the Author

Jo Johnson has been working as a Neuropsychologist for fifteen years. Her specialist interests include brain injury and multiple sclerosis. Previous publications include 'Shrinking the Monster', a workbook for people with MS. This book won a Plain English award in 2009. She has written several books to meet the needs of children who have a parent with a neurological diagnosis, including 'How to Talk to Your Kids about MS', 'My Mum Makes the Best Cakes' and 'My Dad Makes the Best Boats'.

She currently lives and works in Sussex, England.

About the Illustrator

Lauren Densham studied Graphic Design at college before training in Outdoor Pursuits in Scotland. She went on to work in a Special Needs School working with young people with a range of needs and disabilities. She left the post to be a full time Mom.

She currently lives in Warwickshire, England with her husband and baby boy.

CONTENTS

1 :: What's the point of this book?

In this book I have tried to do four things:-

Explain why people change after a brain injury.	Give information about the brain that is easy to understand.
Help you, the reader, to think about ways you can look after yourself.	Talk about personal feelings and why it is so confusing and upsetting living with a parent who has a brain injury.

My aim in writing this book is to allow you as a young person to understand your emotions and feelings on this subject. I also hope it will help you to be able to talk to other people you know about how brain injuries change families and the lives of young people.

"Hi, I'm Josh and I'll be joining you along the way and giving handy tips and advice."

My life changed forever when…

'My Dad nearly drowned.
He survived, but his brain had been starved of oxygen and now his brain is damaged.'

'At Christmas my Dad was ill. He had a headache and was very sick. Later that day he went into a coma. The hospital said he had an infection in his brain.'

'My Dad had a car accident. We were told he had a brain injury.'

'Dad walked me to school as usual but on the way home he was hit by a truck. He was in the hospital for eight months. He broke both his legs and got a head injury.'

'My Mom fell down the stairs when she was carrying the washing. She fractured her skull.'

'My Mom had a brain hemorrhage. The doctors called it a stroke.'

All these things might be described as an acquired brain injury or an ABI.

2 :: What's an ABI?

The term Acquired Brain Injury (ABI) is used to describe all types of brain injury that occurs after birth. The brain can be injured as a result of:

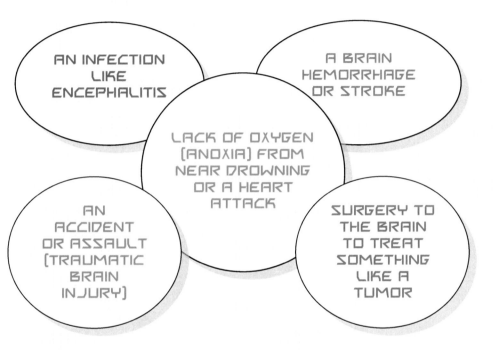

A brain injury involves injuring or damaging the brain.
No surprises there!

The brain controls everything we think, feel and do, as well as how we move, what we smell and what we see. Everything about you is controlled by your brain.

You may be sitting on a chair or on your bed to read this book.
I bet you have not stopped to think what your brain has achieved in just the last few minutes.

Your brain has allowed you to:

Put the words together and understand them.

Remember what books are for and how to recognize them.

Find this specific book in your room.

Pick the book up.

Resist distractions like your Facebook account or IPod.

Keep focusing on the pages.

See the words and understand them.

Make your arms and hands turn the pages.

Keep you from falling asleep.

Keep your body sitting up and not falling over!

Look in the right direction at the book and not out of the window!

Remember each page so you can understand the next page.

So what happens when my brain is damaged?

We are not aware all these things are going on because our brains are working so well. Everything happening is happening subconsciously, meaning that we don't have to think about it at all. However, our brains are in control of everything we do.

So, damage to the brain can create many different changes in someone. Two individuals who have had a brain injury may have a completely different set of symptoms.

The brain is so complex that the best scientists in the world can't really understand how it works, so I am not going to bore you with too much detail.

"There are plenty of online resources you can access if you want to understand it all in more detail. Just ask your science teacher or doctor. Or for all you computer fanatics, simply type 'The human brain' into a search engine on the web. You will find pages and pages of information."

3 :: Facts about the Brain

So what is my brain like?

THE SHAPE OF
A WALNUT

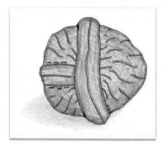

The Size of a
Coconut

The Colour of
Raw Meat

The Texture of
Firm Jelly

The brain is the most powerful organ in the human body and yet it only weighs about three pounds (about the same as nine apples!)

Every day thousands of your brain cells die and cannot be replaced, but don't start panicking. Your brain is overflowing with billions and billions of neurons.

These are nerve cells, used for sending signals inside the brain. Messages from your body, (For example: pain when you get thumped by someone like an annoying brother/sister) rush through your nerves at very high speeds. They travel faster than the fastest car (that is why you feel pain very quickly!)

"Throughout life, especially as children, we bang our heads frequently (e.g., on the bed, falling off the slide, on the car door etc.). Most of the time we don't end up with a brain injury because we have a strong bone structure surrounding and protecting our brain called a skull. The skull is the bony bit which feels hard if you tap your head and is like a 3D jigsaw with over twenty different bones!"

So what's inside my brain?

Well, the brain has three main parts:

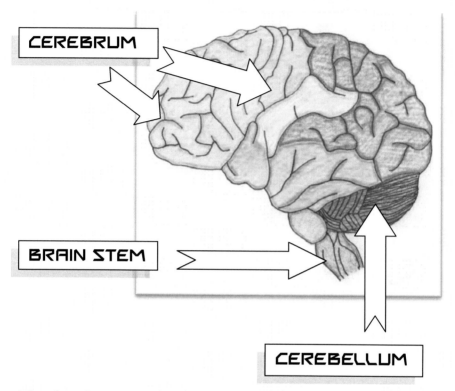

CEREBRUM

BRAIN STEM

CEREBELLUM

The Cerebrum

The **cerebrum** is the large rounded structure of the brain filling most of the skull. It is involved with all the things that make us intelligent human beings like thinking, feeling, remembering, learning, solving problems and behaving in the right way.

It also controls how we move. Different parts of the brain sort out different messages from different parts of your body.

The Brain has two halves called hemispheres. The right half works the left side of the body and the left half works the right side of the body.

In most people, the area for speaking and understanding words is on the left side. These two sides of your brain are joined together by a thick strap of millions of nerves so messages can pass from one side to the other.

"Diagrams like the one on the previous page, make it look as if the parts are like jigsaw pieces, easy to pull apart. In reality the parts are all one color, pink and mushy (not blue, yellow and green!) and it is harder to see where the lobes merge into each other. Have a look on the internet or in a biology textbook to see some pictures of real brains."

Each side or hemisphere has separate parts called lobes. Each half or hemisphere has four lobes called the frontal, temporal, parietal and occipital lobes.

"If you put your hand on your forehead, your hand will cover most of your frontal lobes. These lobes are the biggest and most important part of the brain in humans. Right at the back, at the top of your neck are your occipital lobes. The lobe behind your ear is called the temporal lobe and in between the temporal lobe and the back of the brain is the parietal lobe."

The part of the brain that makes our body parts move is called The Motor Cortex. It is found in the Frontal Lobe. Different parts of the Motor Cortex move different parts of our body.

There is another part of our brain that is next to the Motor Cortex that helps us feel what is happening in different parts of our body. This area of the brain is called the Sensory Cortex and it is found in the Parietal Lobe. The sensory cortex lets your brain know when your friend sticks a needle in your finger.

Cerebellum

The **cerebellum** is at the back of your head, under the cerebrum. It helps us move well and balance, sit down without falling off a chair and pick up a glass of water without spilling it, amongst many other things. Scientists think it also does some remembering and learning how to do things; like riding a bike or unicycle, kicking a ball or playing a musical instrument.

"The Cerebellum looks a bit like a broccoli stalk, probably tastes as bad too!"

Brain Stem

The **brain stem** is under the cerebrum in front of your cerebellum. It connects the brain to the spinal cord (the long bit inside your back bone). The spinal cord connects the brain to the rest of your body.

The brain stem controls all the things we don't think about. Every second the brain sends messages to other parts of your body like the heart, lungs and stomach; to keep you breathing, your heart beating and your stomach rumbling. It is a good thing that we don't have to concentrate on all this stuff or we wouldn't have time to do anything else!

The Limbic System

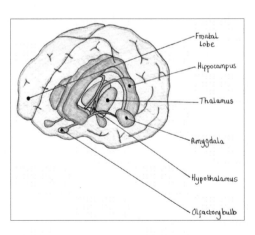

If you cut the brain down the middle between your eyes you can also see some extra bits in the center. An important middle part of the brain is called the limbic system. The limbic system works with the frontal lobes to help us understand our emotions and keep them under control. It is also involved with remembering.

The Pipes

Every time your heart beats, the arteries (blood vessels or pipes!) that carry blood from the heart, take about a quarter of all your blood to your brain. This gives it the oxygen and sugar, which the brain needs to work. It is a bit like gas in a car. A brain injury can happen because of a break or blockage in a pipe. This is sometimes called a stroke or a hemorrhage.

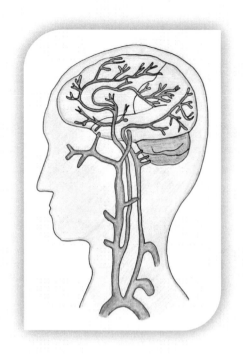

The brain is the hottest part of your body because it needs lots of energy to work well. Have you heard the term 'hot-headed'? Some people call an angry person a 'hot-headed person' but we're all hot-headed!

For many years scientists have tried to work out which parts of the brain do what things. They have found out some things but for the majority of the time, many of the brain parts all work together.

Some brain injuries damage just one part of the brain and a person might have just a few problems but other brain injuries can damage lots of brain parts and the person may have lots of problems.

4 :: After a brain injury – why is everyone so different?

After a brain injury everyone has a different set of problems and gets better in a different way. How someone gets better after a brain injury will be due to three key factors:

> What a person is like before their injury

> What has happened to the brain

> What happens after the injury

1. What the person was like before the injury

We all start off with different brains. We are all individuals. We look different and we have different likes and dislikes. Some people like curry while others like Chinese food. We have different strengths and weaknesses. Some are good at football while others are clever at science. Some people cry if they read a sad story whereas other people never cry but shout a lot. You might have lots of friends and enjoy going out but you probably have a quiet friend who likes to read and hates big groups.

We are even different to our brothers and sisters. As soon as we are born our brain changes with every experience and with every new person we meet.

So by the time somebody is an adult, although each brain has some things the same, (remember the lobes and hemispheres?) everyone's brain has developed differently because of their own family and experiences.

2. What has happened to the brain?

If you fall off a ladder, you will have a different injury than somebody who has had a stroke or a car accident. Different kinds of brain injuries cause damage in different ways. Also the brain may have less damage if the person gets to hospital quickly or is young and healthy.

3. What happens after the injury

After a brain injury everyone goes back to their own individual family and has more new experiences. Everybody has a different life and a unique family. Some people have children while others are divorced. Some people live in a first floor apartment (which helps if your walking is bad) whereas others live in a two-story house.

We have different relationships in our families, some good and some not. Some people are rich while others are not. All these things mean that the experience of your parent after a brain injury will be very different from another person with a similar injury. So...

...EVERY BRAIN IS UNIQUE.

...EVERY BRAIN INJURY IS UNIQUE.

...AND EVERYONE HAS A UNIQUE LIFE.

The symptoms your parent shows will be a mixture of how they were before their injury, the type and amount of damage to the brain and their new experiences after their injury.

5 :: Why has my parent changed?

"My parent is not the same as before their injury…

"He says really weird things."

"My Mom doesn't care if I do my homework anymore."

"My Mom doesn't cuddle me."

"My Dad laughs at my music in a way that upsets me."

"My Dad always looks untidy."

"My Mom looks at me in a different way."

…and people just don't get it!"

"People just don't see how he/she is different."

"My teacher said that my Dad looks really well."

"My friends think Mom is back to her old self."

"They can't see what the brain injury has done."

"I wish my Dad had a stick or guide dog so people would see he is not well."

One of the hardest things about brain injury is that young people often feel that their parent has changed; that the old Mom or Dad has gone and the person now living with them is different. This is made harder because people outside of the family often don't see the changes. It can be frustrating and upsetting when teachers, friends and even relatives think your parent is back to normal when you feel their behavior is anything but normal.

However, this can be made a bit easier by understanding more about the changes that have taken place. These are not in any way your fault but due to the brain injury they have sustained.

We have already looked at how our brains do everything and make us who we are. So, if the brain is damaged, then anything about a person can change.

Changes can be described under these four headings:-

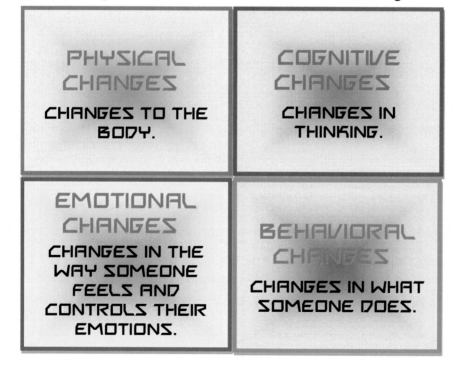

PHYSICAL CHANGES

CHANGES TO THE BODY.

COGNITIVE CHANGES

CHANGES IN THINKING.

EMOTIONAL CHANGES

CHANGES IN THE WAY SOMEONE FEELS AND CONTROLS THEIR EMOTIONS.

BEHAVIORAL CHANGES

CHANGES IN WHAT SOMEONE DOES.

Physical Changes

Physical changes are the easiest to understand. It is when parts of your body do not work or feel as they should. Only about a quarter of people who have had a brain injury have physical problems such as: having a limp, having a weak arm, needing a wheelchair, etc.

Physical changes are in most ways easier to cope with than cognitive, emotional and behavioral changes. Physical changes can be seen and understood by others, whereas cognitive, emotional and behavioral changes are often invisible.

"My Dad has a limp..."

"My Mom wears glasses now..."

"My Mom can't move on one side, her left arm and leg are floppy."

"My Mom can't walk..."

My Dad wears a hearing aid...

Cognitive Changes

You may have already heard people talk about your parent experiencing cognitive changes or having problems with cognition. This is an odd word and is hard to understand or explain.

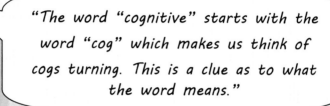

"The word "cognitive" starts with the word "cog" which makes us think of cogs turning. This is a clue as to what the word means."

Some people say that cognition means 'mental ability' or 'thinking'. It is a hard concept to explain and perhaps easier to "do" cognition than explain it!

Imagine you are at School/ College. The teacher asks you a question. "Do cats have four legs?" You put your hand up and give the answer. Think about what you need to do to answer this simple question:

Find your way to the classroom by remembering where you have been before.
Recognize through your eyes what a chair looks like and coordinate your body to sit down.
Select your teacher as the target to focus on.
Stop yourself getting distracted by the good looking person walking past the window or last night's episode of "Doctor Who."
Hear each of the teacher's words and understand what they mean as individual words and as a whole sentence.
Remember what a cat is and what it looks like and then remember that you need to put up your hand in class.
Coordinate this action without hitting your neighbor.
Answer the question with the correct sentence in the right order.

"**WOW**, your brain does all of that without you even realizing, to answer the simplest of questions. All of that is *cognition*."

Scientists like to feel clever so instead of using words like seeing, concentrating, remembering and doing, they use this list of words to describe cognitive abilities:-

Attention - **A bit like concentration, finding the right target. Not getting distracted.**

Visual/Spatial Processing **Recognizing, making sense of things you see.**

Language - **Speaking and understanding.**

Memory - **Remembering facts, things you have done and are going to do.**

Action - **(doing) Learning new things and skills.**

Information processing - **How quickly you can do mental things. How long it takes you to get from the question to the answer.**

Executive Abilities **(see page 25)**

All brain injuries are different and your relative may have problems with one particular cognitive ability, or all of them. They might have only mild difficulties or they might have very big problems.

So what problems are seen with brain injury?

Most people who have had a serious brain injury will experience at least some problems with these four things:

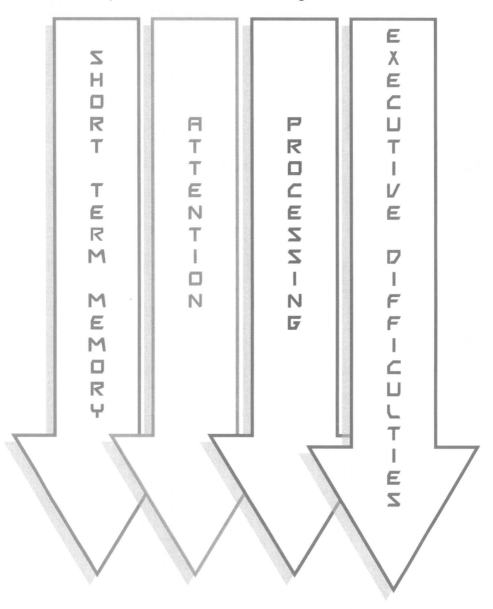

SHORT TERM MEMORY

ATTENTION

PROCESSING

EXECUTIVE DIFFICULTIES

Short Term Memory

After a brain injury people often forget what has happened yesterday or last week, they also forget what they need to do tomorrow. As they forget what you have told them, they repeat the same things and forget to do things they have promised.

Often people who have had a brain injury can't remember the actual accident or when they got their brain injury (perhaps from a stroke or infection.) Your parent may not have any memory of just before or just after the time they got their brain injury. However, they can often remember things from a long time ago, e.g., their childhood, facts they have learned at school, or skills like how to drive, play the piano or ride a bike.

Attention

Psychologists talk about several types of attention; selective, shifting, divided and sustained.

You have to select what to concentrate on (selective attention), listen to your teacher and shift your attention from writing (shifting attention). You then have to divide your attention between two things at the same time, like listening to your teacher and writing notes (divided attention).

"A fly came into the room; the buzzing made her forget what she was saying."

Dad forgets what He is doing if I interrupt him

You may also have to resist distractions in your head e.g., thinking about a party on the weekend or resisting distractions from the environment like the noise other people are making.

You also have to keep concentrating on a task so you don't make mistakes and you get it finished (sustained attention).

"Dad can't cope when I talk when he's watching TV."

"He can't read anymore as he can't concentrate."

People who have had a brain injury usually have problems with all these things.

They can't focus on the right target, get distracted by little things and find it hard to stick to doing something for any length of time.

If attention is difficult, it makes it hard to read a book, watch TV; listen in a group or maybe even cross a busy road. It also means that your parent might get irritable with you if you make too much noise or distract them when they are trying to concentrate on something else.

"Mom was baking a cake and used salt instead of flour!"

Information processing

Information processing is the time it takes you to get from beginning to end in anything you are doing. This could be how long it takes you to make a cup of tea, post a comment on Facebook, answer a question, send a text, complete an algebra question or any other action.

After a brain injury, people can still do lots of things but it takes longer as their cognitive abilities work at a slower pace than before the injury. They also get more easily tired as everything takes so much more effort than it did before. Your parent might seem like they are thinking for ages when you ask them an easy question, a simple form from school might take them a long time to read or complete.

"We have to ask her one thing at a time."

It takes him ages just to send one email now.

"She can't think quickly."

"It takes her so long to answer when I ask to go out..."

Executive Abilities

'Executive abilities' is a very odd phrase. It basically means: How your brain acts as an organizing system. Executive functioning is a complex set of skills controlled mostly by the 'frontal lobes' (remember them?) Managers, (that's the boss) in big companies are sometimes called 'Executives'.

Imagine your school or college.

The young person knows that when they go to school, all the schedules will be ready and the teachers will be in the right place and teaching the right subject (though you may not like it!).

The secretaries will be in the office typing the school reports and calling your parents when you don't turn up for class.

The caretaker will be cleaning the gym for basketball and sweeping the locker rooms.

The janitors are cleaning a room after someone has been sick.

All these jobs have to be done.
The principal is the top manager of the school. He has to know what everyone is doing so that everyone is in the right place doing the right job.

This is like the brain. The brain has many jobs: remembering, learning, moving, seeing and even breathing and digesting too.

> The executive system makes sure all the parts are working together to get the right job done at the right time.

Imagine if...

...all the teachers got their schedules mixed up and the math teacher taught sport and the janitor forgot to clean the gym so people slipped and got hurt.

When the executive system doesn't work, things start to go badly wrong. People remember the wrong things, forget to focus on the right things and speak and move at the wrong time.

Executive abilities allow us to achieve things; to decide to do our homework, find the right book, then focus and finish it. They help us solve a problem or avoid a situation if things are going wrong.

After a brain injury people often have a problem with executive abilities and they might not be able to solve a problem or may be very disorganized and find it hard to get anything done. They often find it hard to make decisions or simply make the wrong ones. Sometimes people think they are lazy or stupid but they are not. It is just the management system in their brain is not working well.

"When I leave for school, Mom is sitting on the chair staring into space. She is still there when I get home."

"Dad keeps getting confused when he tries to cook."

"Dad took me to New York but we were late for the concert as he got the train times in the wrong order."

"I came home from school and my clothes were all over the place. My Mom was trying to tidy my room."

"My Dad starts lots of jobs but never finishes them."

Sometimes he starts doing something then walks away in the middle. Our house is full of half-done jobs.

"My Dad just stares at my homework. He can't think where to start."

If your parent has Cognitive Problems
it might make things easier for everybody if you:

Try not to go too fast. It may be hard for your parent to think quickly. Try not to get frustrated if they need information repeated and check they have understood what you've said.

Pick up your stuff and **try to keep your room tidy** so that your parent doesn't trip and can see things more easily.

Keep important things in an agreed place and put things back in the same place when you use them.

After a brain injury your parent will probably find noise difficult even when it doesn't seem noisy. Try and **keep your music and TV a little quieter** than you are used to. Maybe agree on a set volume that works for both of you.

Help your parent to remember things like school clubs or trips by **getting them to write them down on the calendar** or putting a note on their phone. We remember better if we have something to remind us.

Start a file to put important information in about school, college or social life. Remind your Mom/Dad to check it.

If you want your parent to listen to you or look at something, **wait for a quiet time when you can sit down and focus**. Make sure there are no distractions, so turn off the TV/close the door.

This may all feel **very unfair** to you. Young people are often untidy, noisy and live at a fast pace. This is usual for people of your age. Your friends probably don't have to think about how to help their parent.

It is normal to feel resentful and fed up that you have to think about looking after your parent when parents are supposed to look after you.

"*Make sure you talk to someone about how you are feeling. There are some tips at the end of this book about how to look after yourself which is really important when you have a parent with a brain injury.*"

Behavioral Changes

After a brain injury lots of people show changes in their behavior. Behavior is everything we do. It is hard to say what *normal* behavior is.

Normal behavior changes depending on the situation. For example, it might be normal to swear in front of your friends but not in front of your teachers. Adults might think being untidy is wrong but teenagers feel it is OK.

Normal behavior also depends on the place. It might be ok to wear a bikini on holiday but wouldn't be acceptable at school. Surgeons cut people with knives but anyone else would be sent to prison for doing the same thing!

However, most people agree normal behavior for adults would include:

Doing things for a purpose.

Finishing what they start.

Listening to advice if they can't do things.

Learning from their mistakes.

Saying and doing the right thing depending on who they are with and where they are.

After a brain injury, people tend to show too much behavior or too little behavior:

Too much behavior...

Explosive anger
Getting angry quickly and for a small reason.

Self centeredness
Finding it hard to think about other people.

Rigidity/inflexibility
Wanting everything in a certain way or at the same time and not being able to change quickly and for a small reason.

Irritability
Being grumpy all the time.

Emotional Lability
Crying or laughing very easily or for no real reason.

Disinhibition
Saying things that are rude or not right for the place and person.

Impulsivity
Acting without thinking.

Too little behavior...

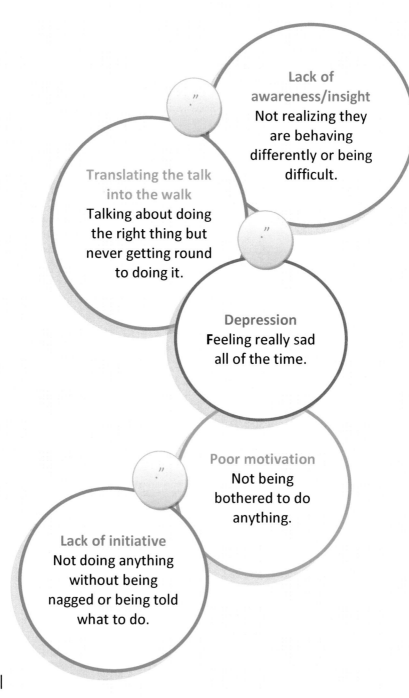

Lack of awareness/insight
Not realizing they are behaving differently or being difficult.

Translating the talk into the walk
Talking about doing the right thing but never getting round to doing it.

Depression
Feeling really sad all of the time.

Poor motivation
Not being bothered to do anything.

Lack of initiative
Not doing anything without being nagged or being told what to do.

Some quotes...

"Sometimes I hate him. He is just not my Dad."

"He shouts at us all the time even when we are good."

"He just sits in the chair all day doing nothing."

"He swears in front of Gran and Mom gets embarrassed."

"She told my teacher about my new bra. It was so embarrassing."

"He thumps the TV even when it is his fault the channel is wrong."

"She shouted at the lady in the shop for not having any bags, I just wanted to die."

Many young people feel that their parent is behaving in an immature way, more like a child than a parent. This is very upsetting, especially as other people don't understand that the changes in behavior are because the brain is damaged and **not** because your parent is rude or a horrible person.

Some young people feel like the parent they first knew has died as the changes after a brain injury make their parent so different. This makes people feel all the things that somebody feels when someone actually dies; sadness all the time, guilt, anger, fear and other feelings that are hard to cope with.

"Make sure you tell someone how you feel.
Your parent is behaving in a changed way
due to the brain injury.
It is not your fault and is not because of
anything you have done."

As we agreed earlier, our brains work so well that most of the time we are not aware of this fact. After a brain injury the person may still be able to do lots of things but many skills that were automatic, (didn't need thinking about) now need lots of effort. It may be more effort for your parent to walk, sit or speak, (all the things we take for granted) as well as all the cognitive abilities we have thought about needing more effort.

This is why people with brain injuries are exhausted all the time and another reason your parent might be impatient, frustrated and short tempered with you.

If your parent has **behavioral problems** the tips below might be useful-

You may need to stop doing something... if your family member is too distressed and frustrated, even if it feels unfair.
Try doing something fun for a while.

Try not to take it personally or get angry... by what your parent is doing, even if it is embarrassing or unkind. It is not your fault.
Do something different.

Keep yourself safe... if your relative is getting very angry. Don't get angry back - it will only make things worse.

Try distraction... If your parent goes on and on about the same thing or says things that are not true, don't get angry with them or tell them they are wrong. Sometimes distracting them can encourage them onto another subject but not always. It is often best to just go into another room or call a friend.

Give your parent as much warning as possible... if you need them to do something so that they have time to think about the situation.

Try to be patient... with your parent if they are getting frustrated by "little things". They are not doing this on purpose and it is probably due to tiredness or their cognitive problems.

Don't try to argue... with your parent about how they may have changed. After a brain injury people cannot always see the changes in themselves. Arguing could make the person frustrated and angry.

Emotional Changes

Look at these pictures and answer the questions next to them.

HOW IS SHE FEELING?

WHAT DOES HE NEED?

HOW DOES HE MAKE YOU FEEL?

It was probably quite easy for you to answer these questions. Most people your age and over can look at other people and know how they are feeling and what to do to help.

We can also understand how we are feeling most of the time. If we are waiting for an exam to start, we feel sick and our heart is racing. We can recognize that we are nervous. If we have the same feeling when we hear a bang downstairs, we know we are frightened that it might be a burglar.

After a brain injury it becomes much harder for a person to recognize their own emotions and to know how others are feeling.

"I feel my dad doesn't care about me. He blanks me a lot."

After a brain injury people are often unpredictable in their moods and can change from happy to angry very quickly, which can be frightening. This is why sometimes your relative seems selfish or insensitive to the needs of other people.

"My Mom cries all the time, I hate it."

We know that if we feel emotional we have to choose who to share it with and where. You probably would not go to your teacher in front of the whole class to tell them how upset you are.

"My Dad cried in front of my new boyfriend."

Sometimes after a brain injury people can't hold in their emotions. This is why your parent becomes emotional with the wrong people or shares private things in front of strangers.

All these changes in behavior and emotions happen because of changes to the brain. This is hard for most of us to understand. If someone has a stroke and the part of their brain that controls walking is damaged, they can't walk.
That is easy to understand.

If they have damage to the parts of their brain that control emotions, personality and behavior, they will experience problems with the way they behave and experience emotions. It is the damage to the brain that makes your parent seem selfish, and behave in a wrong or angry way. It is not their choice and it is not your fault.

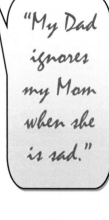

"My Dad ignores my Mom when she is sad."

Your parent may also feel depressed and sad all the time. This is a normal reaction. It is very hard to have a brain injury. They have had to cope with a lot of changes since their injury. A brain injury makes the brain more sensitive and so your parent might cry very easily.

This might be hard for you, especially if it is your dad, or your parent has been somebody who was very unemotional before the accident. Try to understand that your parent may feel sad for a long time after their brain injury. This is not your fault and it is not your job to make them happy again. Often people lose many things. This could be their job or the fact that friends may not visit anymore. They may struggle with not being able to drive or help you with your homework.

Be patient and try to think of fun things to do together when your parent has a good day.

6 :: My family is so different now

Life changes for everyone after a brain injury although it is often the children and young people in the family who notice it most.

Some people feel their family has changed too much. One parent is injured and the other parent is often too busy looking after their partner to have fun. It can seem that family life is all hard work and both parents are no longer around to help. Young people often feel abandoned and lonely.

"I have to do more..."

I have to cook dinner, as Dad gets in late from work and Mom is too tired.

"I have to do all the housework, as Dad is at work and Mom doesn't do it."

"Dad needs me to collect my little sister from school, as Mom forgets."

Lots of young people find they have to help more at home and feel they have less freedom than their friends. Sometimes they also worry about how things are at home when they are out with their friends and this makes life feel less fun.

"We have less money..."

"All my friends went on the school trip to Washington, but we couldn't afford it."

"I had to give up swimming lessons as Dad lost his job."

"We can't afford holidays anymore."

Often if one parent has a brain injury less money comes into the home. Sometimes young people have to give up a hobby like dance class or football as it costs too much money. Others find it hard to get to clubs and see friends, as it is hard to get a ride to where they need to be.

"We had to move out of our house..."

"Dad could not work after his injury so we had to move into a rented house. It is small."

"I had to move to a new area. I miss all my friends."

"We moved, so now I am at a different school. I hate it."

We are moving to a smaller house.

"My Mom had a stroke and could not get upstairs. Now we live in a ranch."

Some young people have to cope with moving to a different school or house. This can be really hard on top of all the other changes after a brain injury.

"I am frightened my parents will get divorced, but sometimes I wish they would so the arguing would stop."

"My parents argue all the time. It makes me stay out more."

"My Mom shouts at Dad even when he is not doing anything."

After a brain injury both parents often feel stressed and upset a lot of the time. It is hard for everyone to cope with all the changes and this can make people less patient with each other and cause them to get angry more quickly.

"My siblings are upset..."

> My brother wets the bed. He is six and my mom thinks it is because of Dad's accident.

> "My brother cries in bed. He misses my Dad, as he is not like our old Dad. I can't help him. I don't know what to do to help anyone."

> "My sister won't help and that makes me angry. She gets away with being selfish because she is doing exams."

It is often hard for the children and young people to see their siblings upset. All families cope in different ways.

Some children and young people show they are upset by behaving differently. Younger children might start doing things they have not done for a long time like crying more, wetting the bed or having big tantrums. Older children might become more withdrawn or start taking their anger out on others in the family or at school- even bullying others. Some teenagers start drinking or staying out late to block out their bad feelings.

This is hard for everyone to cope with and you might feel really worried about your older or younger sibling as well as being worried about your parent.

"My other parent has gone too…"

> My Mom can't take me out, as she has to watch Dad all the time. If he comes out he makes the outing too stressful.

> "My Dad spends every day at the hospital seeing Mom and when we get home from school he just falls asleep."

> "My Mom doesn't want to talk to us about what is going on. She finds it too upsetting."

> "My Dad has a brain injury and my Mom is too tired to care."

> "I have lost my Mom and Dad and no one cares that I am sad too."

When one parent has a brain injury, the other parent is often expected to look after them. The other parent may have to visit the hospital most days or take the injured parent to appointments. It is such a shock when a partner has a brain injury that the other parent is often too upset and tired to be able to think about the children and young people in the family.

Children often have to be cared for by relatives and friends much more than they have been used to. Sometimes this can be fun but often children and young people feel that they have lost both their parents, especially if they have not been used to being cared for by others.

"Strangers come to our house..."

> My Dad has a support worker to help him make lunch. She is nice but it isn't normal, is it?

> "I came home and ten people were in the family room."

> "The OT is teaching Dad how to walk up stairs. It is really annoying."

After a brain injury, some people go to a place or a program where they can do activities or just have a different place to go. This can seem odd for young people who are used to their parent going to work.

> "Everyone else's Dad has a job, mine goes to a day program."

Some parents may stay at home all the time after a brain injury. This may seem strange. Sometimes young people feel they no longer have the space and freedom they had at home before the injury.

After a brain injury, lots of different people might be employed to help your parent. Professionals like physical therapists, occupational therapists, speech therapists, nurses, and aides may all come to your home. They might even have meetings about your parent in your family room. This is really difficult for some young people.

You might feel that your home is constantly full of strangers or that you have to leave the room or be quiet because a parent is having therapy. It is also awkward to bring friends home if you have to explain who these people are and what is going on.

"I miss my old parent..."

> My family is so different.

> "Dad can't walk with us now."

> "My Dad can't kick a football."

> "I miss my Mom taking me shopping."

We talked earlier about people changing after a brain injury. This is often the hardest thing for young people. They may feel they have lost their parent and all the things they used to do with that parent. This is like the feeling people get when someone dies. It is sometimes called grief because it is the feeling you get when you have lost something or somebody important.

Young people often feel like they have lost something after a parent has been injured. They feel their old parent has gone and has lost the ability to do certain activities they used to do.

They may lose their old home, friends or school. This all feels very unfair and it is very normal to feel sad, angry and upset about it all.

7 :: Why am I feeling like this?

'My head feels like a washing machine.
loads of stuff going round and round.
Different colors all tied up in a knot.'

This is how many young people feel when their parent has a brain injury. At first, they often feel happy that their parent is alive or at home, but soon a whole range of other emotions start. Life starts to feel different and they realize that their parent has changed even though they look the same. These are all normal feelings that people feel. Often many feelings come at once or feelings change from one minute to the next. This can make people feel confused.

You may go through all kinds of emotions. You may be sad, worried, or scared. You might be shocked or confused. You might be feeling angry, relieved, guilty, tired, or even empty. Your emotions might be intense, mixed up or just different to anything you have felt before.

Some people find they have trouble learning, sleeping, or eating. Others lose interest in things they used to like. Some people hide themselves away playing computer games or eating or drinking too much. Some people feel as if they are ill. They get stomach pain or feel sick all the time and their body aches all over, while others feel numb, as if nothing has happened.

All of these feelings are normal.

These are some of the things you might think and feel

Shock and Disbelief

"'I feel nothing- numb and frozen."

"I have no idea what is going on."

"I can't believe this has happened to my Dad."

Anger

"Why did this happen to us?"

"Why our family?"

"What did I do to deserve this?"

Grief and Sadness

"I miss my old Mom."

"My Mom doesn't cook anymore."

"My Dad can't do my homework."

Frustration

"I don't know what to do. Life is so difficult."

"I can't do anything I want to do anymore."

Jealousy and Envy

"I wish my Mom gave me as much attention as my Dad gets."

"My friends all have lots more money."

"I wish it was someone else's Dad."

Anxiety and concern

"Will my Mom get hurt?"

"What if my Dad dies?"

"I will fail my exams."

Embarrassment

"My friends think my Dad is odd."

"It is so horrible when he shouts or cries in shops."

"My Dad walks like he is drunk."

Loneliness and Isolation

"No one tells me anything"

"My friends don't understand my old Dad has gone."

Helplessness

"I can't change anything."

"Everyone decides for me."

"I am going to have to change schools, they didn't even tell me until it had been decided."

Resentment

"Our family is rubbish now."

"I don't get any attention."

"I wish he had died."

Never Ending Sadness

"I just want to cry all day."

"I feel life is pointless."

Suicidal Thoughts

"What's the point of living?"

"My life is worthless. I am just another pain for my Mom."

Guilt

"I know she hates me now."

"I wish I could make everything better."

"I can't make my Mom or Dad happy anymore."

One of the things many young people worry about is that the bad things that happen after a brain injury are somehow their fault; that they are somehow to blame for the bad things that are happening. Young people often think these kinds of thoughts:

"Did I cause the accident because of something I said or did?"

"Am I being punished?"

"My parent's difficult behavior is because they don't love me anymore."

All these thoughts are very normal but they are untrue. You did not cause the accident and all the difficult things that happen in families after a brain injury are not your fault. You can't make things go back to the way they were. Some young people feel they should be able to make their parents happy again or feel responsible that their brothers and sisters are sad. You can't make everything better for your family.

It is not your fault that your parent is injured or changed and you can't make them better. It is really important you talk about how you are feeling.

"The important thing about feelings is to share them with someone. All of your feelings are normal, even if you think that they are strange or your thoughts are bad. Other young people will have thought the same things."

Talk to someone in your family or if they are too upset then talk to a teacher, a friend you can trust, a nurse or doctor or anyone you feel comfortable talking to. Don't bottle up your feelings.

Bottled up feelings are like a can of fizzy drink that has been shaken.
In the end they will explode and make a real mess!

8 :: What can I do to look after myself?

A brain injury in the family makes lots of things change and causes everyone in the family to feel lots of difficult things. It is important that you look after yourself well. These are some small things that might help you feel better.

1 Talk talk talk

Talking is a way to get out the bad feelings and to help make others understand what's happening for you. If you can't tell a parent or relative then talk to someone at school. Lots of schools have counselors or at least some kind teachers or favorite coaches. If there's no one to tell, write in a diary.

When people don't talk it is a bit like putting a bandage on a bad wound. At first the bandage covers the cut but it will soon become infected because it is covered and the green pus will ooze out of the bandage edges (yuck!).

When people bottle up feelings, the bad emotions make you ill. Headaches and stomach aches might start. Sometimes people try things like alcohol, drugs or cutting themselves to try and feel better. These things might get rid of the bad feelings for a few hours but soon you have even more problems to cope with.

2 Get active

When you feel sad or upset what you most want to do is nothing!
It is tempting to bury yourself under the blanket, hibernate or disappear.
We know that exercise helps when people feel sad so do something active.

Go for a walk, run or bike ride, play on the Nintendo
dance game with a friend. Do anything that works your
body as we know this releases chemicals in the brain that
make you feel happier. Tell a friend to help you with this.

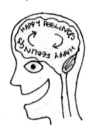

3 Eat well

When you feel sad and upset it can affect how you eat. One person may not
feel like eating at all, but another might eat too much. High fat and sugar
foods like chocolate, chips and crackers are the things you might like to keep
yourself company under the blanket, but these foods make you feel even worse.

Proper food can change the way you feel and give you more energy. So eat
plenty of fruits and vegetables and get regular meals (even if you don't feel
hungry, try to eat something light like a piece of fruit to keep you going.)

4 Remember the good things

We know when people feel sad they are more likely to think about all the bad things and the failures and forget the good things and the times they have done something well. When you have told someone about the bad feelings, try and find some good things to remember.

Try to notice one good thing, and then try to think of one more. Remember the things you are good at and people who are kind to you.

Treat yourself in a kind way: pretend you are your own best friend. Ask a friend or relative to make a list of all the things they like about you or you are good at. Put up the list where you can see it when you are feeling sad.

Find some happy photos to put up with the lists.

Good things
1. Fun to be with
2. Good at listening
3. Relaxed
4. Likes my cooking
5.

5 Keep seeing friends and people who love you

When you feel like rubbish it is easy to stay alone. This will make you feel worse and give you more time to remember the bad stuff. Tell your close friends you need help with this so when you say no to their invitations they will support you to change your mind.

6 Do fun things

Find something you enjoy. Take up a new hobby or get a friend to try a new club with you. Find something that makes you laugh out loud: a comedy show or film, a good book or just having a good time with a friend. Keep doing the good things.

Don't give up things you enjoy because of what is happening at home. Sometimes after a parent has a brain injury it is harder to get rides to places and your family might have less money.

If you need help sorting out the practical things like how to get to a club or how to pay for an activity, etc. ask a teacher at school to help you find a way of doing things you like without your parents having to worry.

7 Sleep

Did you know that staying awake for two weeks could kill you? We know the body and the brain both need sleep to work well and stay healthy. Try and get into a sleep routine and as much as possible go to bed and get up at the same time. Chocolate, smoking and soda all keep you awake so don't have too much of these in the evening.

Make sure your room is dark and quiet and plan some quiet time before you go to bed. Have a notebook by your bed to write down any random thoughts that are keeping you awake.

8 Learn how to calm yourself

Chilling out in front of the TV or computer isn't true relaxation. Some games or programs can even make you more uptight. The same is true for alcohol, drugs, or cigarettes. People tell you they will calm you down but it's a false state of relaxation that disappears quickly then makes you feel worse than you did before.

What the body really needs is a relaxation technique like deep breathing. This has a physical effect on the brain and the body. Deep breathing helps to relax a major nerve that runs from the diaphragm to the brain, sending a message to the entire body to let go and loosen up. Deep breathing has also been shown to improve concentration and make thinking clearer.

Learn how to slow down your breathing. Sit or lie down in a comfortable position. Put on some nice music and just concentrate on taking long deep breaths in and out. Push out your stomach to make your clothes feel tight around your waist and then breathe in as you count slowly to four. Breathe in for four and out for four.

Practice this for ten minutes each day. At first it will be hard but it is like any skill, you will soon get better. When you are really good at this, you will start to notice when your breathing gets too fast. This is a sign you are getting stressed. Find a quiet corner wherever you are to do some deep breathing.

9 Get some fresh air every day

Being outside will make you feel better. Go for a walk, bike ride or sit in the park and take time to really notice what is happening. We are always in a rush and we don't notice what things smell like, or look like, or what is around us.

Take time to really concentrate on what is around you. Some studies have shown that fully concentrating on one thing at a time whatever it is makes you feel happier.

10 List the things you want to change

Ask a teacher or friend to help you think about ways of changing the things you can change and what problems you need to solve. Let an adult know what help you need.

"It is hard to think clearly when there is so much going on in your family. Talk to someone you can trust about which ideas on the last few pages might help you."

9 :: When you must see a doctor

Young people are in the middle of a time in life when the body and brain are changing very fast. When puberty begins around eleven or twelve, the body starts producing sex hormones. These hormones cause physical changes in the body, but they also seem to cause emotional changes and many young people find that their emotions are more mixed up than usual.

It is very normal to experience these emotional ups and downs in the teenage years, but much harder when your parent has a brain injury and your whole family is experiencing lots of difficult emotions.

> **Some young people might become clinically depressed.** This is when someone feels sad or anxious all the time. Life does not feel worth living and there are no happy days. If you feel like this most of the time for more than a couple of weeks you may be suffering from depression, also called clinical depression.

Most people don't really understand depression. Adults might think the person is being lazy or not trying. Some think that depression is just a mood that all teenagers have. Lots of people say they feel depressed when they mean they are feeling fed up.

Sometimes even the young person who is suffering does not realize they are ill. Some feel that they are weak or stupid in some way because they are depressed. This is wrong and makes people hide their feelings and not get help. Sometimes young people who are depressed might see a doctor for other reasons like headaches or stomach pain.

Another common problem some young people might experience is an anxiety disorder. This is when you feel worried most of the time even when you can't think of specific reasons to feel worried. You might experience what is called a panic attack. A panic attack is a feeling of not being able to breathe. Often, people sweat, feel faint and their heart feels as if it is going too fast.

Some young people develop what are called obsessions or compulsions. They might start counting a lot, washing their hands, or develop habits like needing to say goodbye to a parent five times every time they leave. Some people worry that if they don't do these habits something bad will happen. Other young people become very focused on food. They might stop eating and lose a lot of weight or eat all the time and gain weight. Some people use alcohol or drugs to try and block out the pain.

All of these things are very common ways of coping with a stressful situation and a parent with a brain injury can make a situation very stressful.

The important thing to remember is that lots of young people are feeling like you and you can get help to make things better.

You must ask for help from a teacher, counselor or doctor if:

You have thoughts of killing yourself.

You have panic attacks.

You are avoiding things you used to do or places you used to go.

You are cutting yourself, drinking alcohol or taking drugs to block out the pain.

You feel like life is not worth living.

You have problems getting to sleep or staying asleep.

Everything feels pointless.

You can't be bothered to see your friends or do the things you usually like doing.

You have gained or lost a lot of weight.

You don't care as much about your appearance.

You cry most days.

You feel you have no one to talk to.

You are developing habits that you feel you must do, like counting, washing or repeating things.

You feel worried all the time.

10 :: Can anything good come out of my situation?

All changes bring bad things and good things. When a parent has a brain injury it is a huge change, maybe the biggest change you will ever have to cope with. We have thought about the bad things, the things people lose and the ways a parent might change in a way that you don't like. Changes also bring good things.

"We are closer as a family."

""My Mom has more time with me now that she can't work."

"I made a new friend at the hospital."

"My Dad is around more."

"I have learned how to play cards with my Dad."

"My brother and I have to work together."

"The OT explained about her job. I think I might like to be an OT."

"I am close to my Gran who I did not talk to before."

Some studies have looked into what happens when young people become adults; young people who have lived with someone who has a brain injury or a physical disability and young people who have not had this experience. The good news is that lots of young people who have to cope with challenges in their childhood end up gaining positive benefits from their experience. There is some evidence that they:

11 :: Other young people's stories

Alec's Story

"I was 12 years old and just about to start high school when my Mom was taken to the hospital. She was in her early forties and was fit and healthy, so it came out of the blue. The doctors later told us she'd had a stroke and it turned my life upside down. It was very confusing at first and I felt that nobody was explaining to me what was going on. She was in a nursing home for a number of years and during this time, my sister and I both went to a boarding school, as we had no other family who could look after us. I found this very difficult and the first year still seems a complete blur to me. I was bullied and didn't get along with the other kids who had come from very different backgrounds.

When she first came home, it was very strange because so much time had passed since I had seen her before the stroke. I had not really seen her much in the nursing home. It was as if I had forgotten what she was like. This is still something I struggle with today and when I watch videos of her before she was ill, it's like watching another person, although I know it's still her. It was as if my old Mom had died, but had been replaced by a new Mom who looked the same but couldn't talk. However, she still has her wicked sense of humor and is very stubborn. It's the little things like this that remind me she is still the same person.

I still find it difficult to come to terms with what happened to my Mom and how it affected me. I'm not sure if it is possible to ever completely achieve this. However, I do find it is much easier to talk about now. I don't think I coped particularly well at the start, as I think I went through a long period of pretending it hadn't happened. Sometimes I feel I almost acted as if she had died completely. Everybody copes with things differently and this was just what I did in order to help me through.

I can now see that there are many ways in which what has happened to me has had a positive experience in my life. While what happened to my Mom was incredibly tragic and affected me greatly, I am now able to see how appreciative it has made me of everything else. I was lucky to have a really good group of friends who helped keep my life as normal as possible (whatever that is!), but also learned life lessons through shared experiences that my Mom would have otherwise been there to help with.

Some people might go their whole lives without ever experiencing loss and when they do, at say, the death of a pet dog, they do not know how to cope and may break down. I now understand that these things do unfortunately happen, but I am a firm believer in the saying, "What doesn't kill you makes you stronger". When my friends ask me what it was like to be a young caregiver and how I coped with my experience, I can tell them it was hard growing up without my Mom, but I didn't really ever know any different and as a result, that was normal for me.

I have learned to be very independent and am able to get things done for myself when a lot of other people my age can't. I know my Mom is very proud of me and my sister, even if she can't say so herself. Our experiences in life make us who we are and one thing I am sure of is that I would never be where, or more importantly who, I am today if it wasn't for my Mom's stroke. The biggest thing I've learned from the whole situation is that, as long as you always concentrate on the good things, you will always move forward and get the most out of life."

Harriet's Story

"My Mother had a brain hemorrhage. She is hemiplegic which means she is unable to move the right side of her body.

My Mom has a condition called aphasia which means she is unable to say what she is thinking or read a sentence aloud and make sense of it. If you asked her for a spoon, she might pass you a knife or the cat or something. Sometimes she also jumbles up names. Her most common phrase is "the nothing", which she usually says when she has given up explaining what she was trying to say.

When I was younger I felt like she was very angry a lot of the time. She had very little patience and was waiting to wake up and be herself again. Now I'm a little older she has settled a little better. Part of her condition means she has no concept of money and spends too much. If you tell her she can't have something, it results in a child-like argument.

When she can't get her words out she becomes either determined like she's on a mission or she won't speak to anyone. I think she finds the frustration hardest.

It was always my Mom, my brother and me. After the stroke, I guess it was the doll's house effect, letting all these people into our home and life, e.g., social workers and therapists.

When I was little I was very hung up on how much of a brat I was towards my Mom. In fact, I seem to remember that an argument was one of the last full talks we had. I wanted to do everything around the house and be told I was a good girl for helping. When I went to school, I hated getting in trouble because I was worried - I don't really know about what, but it worried me. I used to get bullied but I think all of it made me a stronger person.

I'm a very anxious person these days. I apologize a lot, which I get a lot of comments about and I've got a very short temper. I mainly worry about my Mom, and money. Otherwise, my life is really good. It's always difficult to find people you can trust. They go and someone else comes but I've learned that there's always someone ready to listen, even if it's just to let off some steam. I have found things that I really enjoy and kept myself happy and active. "

Jack's Story

"My Dad had a crash. He was on his motorbike and a car was driving home and crashed into him. My Mom told me that Dad was in the hospital. He had a broken leg and his head was damaged.

He was in the hospital for a month. The day he came home, we decorated the house with balloons, we were so happy he was home. He came in the door and swore at my Gran for putting her shoes in the way. My Mom was crying. I kept thinking my Dad would soon go back to how he was before his crash but he didn't.

He used to read with me and watch DVDs. Now he says it makes his head hurt. We can't play football as he has a limp. He has gotten really fat, as he can't play sports and I think this makes him angry. He is angry a lot and he shouts at all of us even when we are good. Sometimes I hate him. My Mom cries a lot and I know she misses my old Dad too.

Sometimes he is a bit like he was, he laughs at silly jokes and my friends like him, as he kids around as much as us. We are all getting used to the new Dad and sometimes I forget how it was before. My Mom says he has a brain injury and that makes him horrible sometimes, but he doesn't mean it and can't help it.

My teacher at school is helpful and she talks to me when I look sad. My friends are nice to me and we go to their houses more than mine so it is not too noisy for my Dad. I am good at football and my Dad comes to watch and cheers me on, though sometimes he shouts too loud which makes me cringe. I still like him coming."

Tally's Story

"In early 2003, my Father was in a car accident which resulted in a serious brain injury. He was in a coma for three weeks, and even though I was only six, I can remember almost everything from the moment the police arrived to inform my Mom of the accident.

Each member of my family's experience has been and is unique and difficult because my aunts, grandparents, brother and Mom each had a different relationship with my Dad before his accident. We each feel we have lost something. Yet despite the multiple strains and stresses our family has faced, I do feel we have become stronger for them.

Although I struggled in middle school, I am lucky to now have amazing friends who are not only willing, but want to understand. A lot of my friends also have family issues like us, which means we can support each other.

One of the difficult aspects of brain injury is that it can sometimes feel like you've lost someone, and yet they are still there, only changed. My Dad cannot be like other Dads. His emotions and behavior are similar to those of a young child, as opposed to having the same control as an adult. This can be difficult as he can get frustrated, tired or easily upset. However, he is still capable of cracking a good joke and flickers of his old self can be seen. He still maintains his intelligence although he is unable to work anymore, which is sometimes frustrating for him.

I sometimes try to explain my Dad's injury by saying that it's like areas of his personality have been suppressed and other areas have been exaggerated.

I love my Dad very much and even though our lives are quite complicated, I am extremely grateful and particularly proud of my Dad for fighting through."

It's about you too – Your Story

In this last section there are some pages for you to write on. You don't have to do it (it's not like homework), but it might help you make sense of what has happened to your family and think about how you are feeling.

When you have written down what feels important to you, it might be a good idea to show this section to someone you trust- a parent, relative or teacher, and ask them to help you think about any changes that can be made to help you. It is important that you get all the right information and support you need.

What happened to your parent?

Write any questions you have about the brain.

Does your parent have any physical difficulties?
e.g., a limp

Have you noticed any cognitive problems your parent has? If so write some examples. (e.g., memory loss)

Have you noticed any changes in the way your parent behaves or changes to their personality? (e.g., getting angry easily) How do these changes make you feel?

Has you parent changed in the way they understand or use emotions? (e.g., crying easily)
What changes have you noticed?

What are the changes that have happened in your family that you find most difficult? Write these changes here and ask an adult you trust to help you think of ways to make these things feel better.

What feelings have you had since your parent's injury? How are you feeling now? Who can you talk to about these feelings?

Look back over the section, "What can I do to look after myself". What can you do to make yourself feel even a little better?

Are there any things that you are doing that are not helping? Look at the list of things that would mean you must seek help (when you must see a doctor). Are there things on that list that you do? Write them below. You must seek help from an adult so you can get the right help to make things feel better.

Finally, are there any good things that would not have happened if your parent had not had a brain injury?

12 ::Further help

Hopefully some of your questions have been answered in this book. If you have other questions or you need further help and support, here are the details of some good places to start looking:

National Organizations

> ## Brain Trauma Foundation
> www.braintrauma.org

> ## The Brain Injury Association of America (BIAUSA)
> www.biausa.org

> ## Centers for Disease Control and Prevention – Traumatic Brain Injury
> www.cdc.gov/ncipc/factsheets/tbi.htm#top

> ## National Association of State Head Injury Administrators
> www.nashia.org

> ## United States Brain Injury Alliance
> www.usbia.com

Resources for veterans with brain injuries and their families:

Military One Source
www.militaryonesource.mil

Hope for the Homefront
www.hopeforthehomefront.com

Make the Connection (For Veterans)
www.maketheconnection.net

Wounded Warrior Project
www.woundedwarriorproject.org

Books and Resources:

Lash and Associates Publishing/Training Inc.
www.lapublishing.com

Brain Injury Blog
www.lapublishing.com/blog

'My Mom had a brain hemorrhage. The doctors called it a stroke.'

'At Christmas my Dad was ill. He had a headache and was very sick. Later that day he went into a coma, the hospital said he had an infection in his brain.'

Young people in families changed by brain injury are often the forgotten victims. At a time of trauma and uncertainty, they are frequently left feeling upset and confused.

'My Parent has a Brain Injury' gives factual information about brain injury. It provides information to reassure young people about the wide range of feelings they might be experiencing, as well as strategies to help them deal with these emotions. It also offers clear guidance and information about organizations that offer help and support to young people in these situations.

This book has been written in a clear and colorful way that will appeal to young people across a wide range of ages.
It can be used as a standalone resource or to support individual or group work in clinical or home settings.

'My Dad had a car accident. We were told he had a brain injury.'

'An excellent book that will be a source of support for many young people.'
Headway - The Brain Injury Association

"This is an innovative and creative new book which will help young people and provide coping strategies at a very difficult time.'
Brain Injury Rehabilitation Trust (BIRT)

'I realised I was not the only person feeling rubbish and stressed.' *Phoebe, 14*

'My husband had a head injury six years ago. I wish this book had been around then to give to my children.'